Practical help for your church in the
Decade of Evangelism

Reaching Young Families

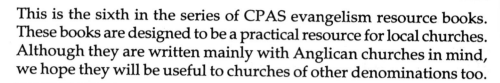

Using this Book

This is the sixth in the series of CPAS evangelism resource books. These books are designed to be a practical resource for local churches. Although they are written mainly with Anglican churches in mind, we hope they will be useful to churches of other denominations too.

What about copyright?

This material may be photocopied without charge for use in talks and discussion groups provided the © CPAS copyright notice is retained on each page.

CPAS places no formal restrictions on the number of copies made, but to permit the publication of further resource materials we recommend that each leader of a group purchases his or her own copy of this book.

This book is intended as a tool for all those in a church with responsibility for Parent and Toddler groups: not only the leaders and helpers charged with the day to day running of the group, but also those with a more general oversight. It is aimed at all who share a concern for reaching out to young families through friendship and practical service.

It can be read by individuals like any other book, but its main purpose is to encourage a 'whole church' strategy for facilitating and developing the contribution of the Parent and Toddler group. Often we fail to make the most of the many contacts created through this popular (and frequently overlooked) form of service. The book's photocopiable resources should provoke discussion and decision making on the vital task of building bridges between the local church and its surrounding community.

What's what?

The resource material falls into five sections, each with some or all of the following:

 An *Introduction* page which outlines the contents of the section. It also gives extra group activities and ideas on how to use the materials.

 A *Briefing* paper on the theme of the section. This is either for a leader's own information or for photocopying and distribution to members of a planning group or church council.

 One or more *Discussion* papers for group members. Again, these are designed for photocopying; they may not refer directly to the briefing papers and so may be used on their own.

 A collection of *Ideas* to provide starting points for discussion and planning.

 One or more *Illustrations* for talks or group work. They may contain cartoons or graphics. These illustrations may be photocopied on to acetate sheets for use with an overhead projector.

Is it a course?

The material has not been set out as a five-part course. However, group leaders may wish to select from the briefings and discussion papers and put together their own series of sessions to help them focus on practical strategies for making the most of their group's contacts and opportunities.

Stepping Out

Contents

 A two page *Briefing* paper outlining the unique role and special opportunities of Parent and Toddler groups.

 A *Discussion* paper based on a study of Mark 6:30-46.

 A *Discussion* paper to help group leaders focus on the joys, pressures and problems of caring for small children in the 1990s.

 An *Ideas* research project to help you assess the current level of provision for under fives in your area.

Extras

Resources

The Pre-school Playgroup Association is an invaluable source of practical guidance. The following publications are particularly recommended:

Guidelines—Good Practice for Parent and Toddler Playgroups (PPA 1990)

Running a Parent and Toddler Playgroup (PPA 1992)

Available from: PPA National Centre, 61-63 Kings Cross Road, London WC1X 9LL
(071) 833 0991

Playleader Magazine. Published three times a year by Diana Turner, *Playleader* aims to link Christians working with preschool children. It is available on subscription of a suggested annual donation of £3.00.

Playleader, 125 Finchfield Lane, Wolverhampton, West Midlands WV3 8EY
(0902) 763108

Focus on Children

How do small children think? How do they believe and how does their faith develop?

Penny Frank's *Children & Evangelism* (Marshall Pickering) provides a useful way in to understanding what makes children tick. See page 40 for more details.

Stepping Out

Groups for adults and children are making an impact: 'Slightly more than one church in six is now offering this kind of facility and making contact with around 77,000 children under the age of six. A significant aspect of the work of these groups is among the parents. There are two present for every three children.' (*Children in the Way*, National Society / Church House Press, 1980)

Serving young children and their carers together.

Exploring potential for evangelism.

Bringing them over the threshold is just the beginning of the task.

Four years ago I wrote *Under Fives and their Families* (Marshall Pickering / CPAS, 1990). It included a chapter on Parent and Toddler groups. These were one of several types of pre-school groups considered in the book as a valuable base from which effective Christian witness to parents and children could take place. Judging by the response I received, it proved to be the most thoroughly read of all the chapters.

What are Parent and Toddler groups?

Take the basic ingredients: small children aged 0-5 years in areas with limited nursery and playgroup provision, but more commonly 0-2½ years. Add their accompanying adults: select from mums, grannies, childminders, dads or foster-parents. Combine with a team of dedicated helpers from a local church. Mix thoroughly in the venue of your choice: church hall, scout hut or large living room. Season with toys, games, songs and stories. Keep the mixture simmering through a regular programme of morning or afternoon sessions...

It's a highly popular recipe, currently being used to good effect in hundreds of places and under almost as many names. Titles include the informal (Coffee'n'Kids, Jack and Jill, Playtime, Squeals on Wheels), the biblical (Noah's Ark) and the frankly optimistic (Little Angels).

Trying to find a name that describes the clientele accurately can prove difficult. 'Mums and Toddlers' now seems too narrow a focus; and while the initials ABC (Adults, Babies and Children) and ABT (Adults, Babies and Toddlers) are more accurate, they are not yet as well known as the more traditional 'Parents and Toddlers'.

This last is the name that will be used in this book. It's not perfect but it has the advantage of being widely recognized. Also it conveys the spirit of these groups where the majority of adults are parents, though not necessarily of the child they are accompanying.

But while names differ, all these Parent and Toddler groups have a common core: they aim to serve young children and the adults who care for them *together*. In contrast to nurseries and playgroups, offering a 'drop-off' service is not part of their brief. Parents *and* Toddlers—these are the groups at which this book is aimed.

The purpose of this book

First, what this book is not:

• It is not a guide to the setting-up and day-to-day running of a Parent and Toddler group. Other agencies and publications offer step-by-step guidance on vital issues of insurance, safety and hygiene. This book won't tell you how to meet the legal requirements of the Children Act (1989).

Instead, this book aims to be the following:

• A resource for church-linked Parent and Toddler groups which want to develop their potential for evangelism in the local community. It

offers ideas, suggestions and discussion-starters but no prescriptions. It is formula-free!

It makes three important assumptions about Parent and Toddler groups:

- They are an integral part of the Christian witness of the whole church and not independent or isolated units. As such they are valued, supported and accountable.

- Their basic motivation is one of service, a desire to demonstrate the love of God in the community by offering support and friendship to young children and their carers.

- Through their contacts and friendships they will pray and seek for opportunities to bring greater understanding of God, knowledge of the gospel and response to Jesus Christ.

Meeting the need

There appears to be no shortage of enthusiasm for setting up Parent and Toddler groups. Increasing numbers of churches are grasping the unique opportunities that such groups provide in bringing tens, sometimes hundreds of adults and children across the threshold of a church building into contact with Christian people. What could be more exciting and challenging in a Decade of Evangelism? I know of no other area of church life that succeeds in this task in quite the same way. But, as many of us involved in running such groups know, bringing them over the threshold and establishing the initial contact is just the beginning of the task.

What are Parent and Toddler groups aiming for?

The recurring question I am asked is, 'How, once we have established contact with people, can we move them on?' Moving people on from that initial point of contact in a Parent and Toddler group to an increasingly re-sponsive understanding of God is the goal we set ourselves. Our sights seem set, but actually achieving that goal appears to be difficult.

How do we move people on?

The moving on process rarely happens overnight. It is more likely to occur over period of time. Over many years of working in Parent and Toddler groups I have become aware of a very definite pattern emerging. It can be helpful to see this pattern as stages in the developmental process:

- Building relationships.
- Dispelling myths people have been told about God and the Church.
- Being prepared to share your positive experience of God.

These three stages are critical and take time. We shall look at them more closely in the following chapters. Experience has taught me that short cuts lead to short-circuiting! Everybody's journey will be unique.

How do Parent and Toddler groups aid that journey?

It is the unique circumstances of Parent and Toddler groups that create one of the best environments for preparing the ground for spiritual searching and growth. The informal setting, the sharing of common interests and experiences and the frequency of meeting can't help but encourage sharing of lives and faith. Parent and Toddler groups make three very considerable achievements:

- They meet a need in the lives of individuals and their wider community.

- They provide a vital bridge to promote mutual understanding.

- They provide an environment in which faith can be shared naturally and meaningfully.

Each of these areas is explored in more depth in the following chapters.

Parent and Toddler groups create one of the best environments for preparing the ground for spiritual searching and growth.

Stepping Out

 Notes

A task too big?

Read Mark 6:30-46

People have needs—physical, emotional, spiritual. No one understood that better than Jesus. His insight was profound. His compassion was practical.

Read the passage twice. First in silence, individually. The second time allocate a narrator, a reader of Jesus' words and several people to read the disciples' words. Now read the passage aloud using the different voices.

The need

- Even though Jesus was tired and hungry, what was it that made him stay and speak to the crowd?
- In what ways are families with young children in the 1990s like 'sheep without a shepherd'?
- Write down some of the fears and anxieties that adults have for themselves and their children.

A problem

- *Verses 36 and 37* Who identified the problem?
- What was the disciples' solution to the problem?
- What spoken and unspoken objections do you think they had to Jesus' solution?
- In what ways are we in danger of telling God what to do when the task feels too big?
- Be honest about any feelings of inadequacy you might have for the task of reaching out through Parent and Toddler groups. When God says to us 'You do it', how can we respond honestly to him?

A solution

- *Verse 38* The disciples eventually listened to Jesus and did as he asked. *Verses 42-44* He took the little that they had and used it to meet the needs of the people.
- Lack of leaders and facilities are the most commonly identified objections to starting or developing a Parent and Toddler Group. Make a list of all that you have at the moment and prayerfully work out what you are able to offer God in terms of time, energy and resources.
- *Verse 46* Jesus was tired at the start. What did he do at the end?
- Discuss practical ways in which you can spend time in prayer, individually and corporately, both listening and talking to God about your Parent and Toddler group.

Stepping Out

Notes

Changing Times

The aim of this group exercise is to help you focus on the needs of young families today. Comparing our current situation with that of our parents and grandparents can give a helpful perspective on changing needs and expectations.

Part one

Think about the everyday practicalities of caring for pre-school children. In small groups discuss and compare the lifestyle of your family nowadays with what you know and remember about the recent and not so recent past.

Think about your parents' circumstances (housing, income, support services) when they were caring for small children.

Next discuss your grandparents' lifestyle when they were at that stage.

- What changes do you personally welcome?
- What aspects from the past would you personally like to have retained?

Part two

Greater freedom is often accompanied with a mixture of joy, confusion and guilt. Discuss the influences and effects upon young families in your community that the following changes have brought:

- Modern labour-saving devices for the home—everything from microwaves to vacuum cleaners and dishwashers.
- Increased opportunities for work and career development for women.
- Separation, divorce and the choice of 'non-marriage' between couples.
- Breakdown of extended family networks, with many people now living long distances from relatives.
- Changing values and increased crime rate in society.

- Do we have too much?

Part three

Change, whether we like it or not, is here to stay!

- How can your Parent and Toddler group become a support to young families struggling in the face of society's changing times?
- Decide together what are the three most important things that a Parent and Toddler group can provide in the face of some of these changes.

Stepping Out

There has been rapid increase in the provision for pre-schoolers and their carers in the last ten to fifteen years. Local authorities and private establishments have woken up to the fact that there is a market for this important section of the community.

Church members thinking of establishing Parent and Toddler groups would do well to research the facilities available in their area. Doing so will help them learn from the experience and expertise of others. It will also prevent them from duplicating valuable work. While the spiritual goals of a church-based group will be unique, we need to remember that the initial point of contact in the community is found in meeting the practical and social needs of the people.

The questions opposite are to help you in your local research, the results of which should enable you to provide an effective and much needed Parent and Toddler group.

Draw all this information together. Use it to write your own brief 'mission statement' for your group.

Make sure it answers the basic questions:

- Why are we running a Parent and Toddler group?
- Who are we running it for?
- What are we aiming to do?

Local Research Action Plan

1 What nursery and playgroup provision is available in your area?

Find out about locations, days, times and age groups of children received. Make a note of the demand for these facilities (find out about numbers on waiting lists). Take all of this information into account in the planning of your own groups.

2 Which of the following services are available in your area?

- Community-based Parent and Toddler groups.
- Special library sessions for under fives.
- Special leisure centre activities (swimming, gymnastics etc) for small children.
- Visits from a playbus.
- Toy libraries.
- National Childbirth Trust support groups.
- Play facilities in local parks.
- Local museums, country parks, open farms and other attractions that make special provision for young children and their carers.
- Child minders' support network.

3 What lessons can you learn from these services in terms of publicity, cost, timing and facilities?

4 Look back at your church's history of provision for under fives and their families.

What has been offered in terms of Sunday school, crèche, playgroups, pram services or informal meeting points for parents and small children? Has there ever been a Parent and Toddler group? Find out about who initiated them and why? Did they fulfil their intended purpose? Why did they finish? What lessons can be learned from their experience?

5 Decide together who exactly your group is aiming to serve.

- Are you placing any limitations according to sex: are men welcome?
- Or according to the type of carers: are child-minders and grandparents welcome?
- Or according to locality: will the group be 'open access' or will you have a specific catchment area?
- Are you making the most of contacts the church already has with families from baptism and thanksgiving services?
- What about contacts through local midwives or health visitors?
- Or perhaps there is one particular housing estate where several church folk live for which the church has a particular concern.

Building Relationships

Contents

 A three page *Briefing* paper on building quality relationships.

 A *Discussion* sheet on Parent and Toddler group leadership.

 Two *Discussion / Ideas* pages on welcoming adults and children into a group.

 An *Ideas* page for setting up special events for the members of your group.

Extras

Learning to Listen

Any Parent and Toddler session is a mixed community of different ages, backgrounds and needs. The quality of our service will be closely linked to the skill and sensitivity with which we listen to each individual in the group.

Use this list for a quick check-up on the current state of your listening skills.

- **Listening to God.** The most important form of listening—when you pray, who does all the talking?
- **Listening to friends and neighbours.** Hearing what people say is easy enough, actively listening is more of a challenge. Listening to what is unspoken takes great sensitivity.
- **Listening to children.** Really listening to what small children are trying to say takes conscious effort, insight and a lot of patience.
- **Listening to myself.** Taking into account one's own feelings can often be the key to listening to others.

Leadership: getting the balance right

'With strong administrative back-up our own group aims for three leaders to 25 parents on the register. In practice this rarely reaches more than 21 or 22 due to sickness, holidays etc. Wherever possible we have at least one of those leaders with no children of their own so that they are free to handle a crisis and give undivided attention wherever it is required. One leader handles registration, another the daily activity leaving the third to 'float'. If we are all absorbed in a whirlwind of activity we cannot hope to build up any friendships.' (Judith Wigley, *Under Fives and their Families*, Marshall Pickering)

How does this picture match up to the day-to-day reality of your group?

Discuss ways you can make the most effective use of your current level of leadership.

Building Relationships

Two identical booths selling delicious ice cream stood just ten yards apart in the central square of the Spanish village in which we were staying. Their selection and prices were the same but we always went to the same one. Why? Quite simply because the Senora serving there was a smiling, happy, friendly woman who made our daily trip a very enjoyable experience! She smiled patiently at our feeble attempts to speak Spanish, gently encouraging and correcting us as we did so, until we found the children eagerly practising in preparation for this daily visit. We had quite a relationship going by the end of our holiday and if we ever return I feel sure that she will be among the first people we shall look for.

Priority to relationships

Relationships are the blood vessels of life in our Parent and Toddler groups. Shops, stores and large companies spend thousands of pounds training their employees in the art of developing good customer/client relationships. Their motivation is to sell, to make a profit. Ours is to share something of the very best relationship of all – with the Son of God.

So often the lives of Christians have become insular and detached from the reality of ordinary non-Christians' lives. The endless pressure of church activities leaves little time for simply being a good neighbour and befriending those around us. We have lost, or perhaps never developed, the desire and skills required to build good relationships.

Parent and Toddler groups provide the ideal environment and circumstances in which to cultivate friendships for God. Quality relationships with both adults and children will encourage a natural sharing of lives. Part of this, for the Christian, will involve sharing his or her experience of God.

There are very many practical things that can be done in order to begin to build these relationships. Too often we fail to recognize the natural opportunities provided in Parent and Toddler groups.

> 'Children and parents need to feel that they belong and are loved in a group. We should make sure we know them by name, welcome them, and spend time with them. We should listen to them and talk to them about the things that matter to them: a child's new shoes, illness in the family, sleepless nights.'
>
> (Sue Kirby, *People Jesus Met*, CPAS, 1991)

Welcome to our group!

Many first-time parents, grannies and even childminders make their first visit to a Parent and Toddler group with fear and trepidation not knowing what to expect. The fact that the group is church-based will serve only to increase their levels of anxiety and suspicion. First impressions are lasting ones and there is no more critical time in the process of building a relationship than that point of initial contact with an adult and child as they walk through the door of a group for the first time. The welcome that we give, the way in which we present details about the running of the group and how well we succeed in integrating them into the existing circle is of the utmost importance.

The 'welcome procedure' should always be conducted on a one-to-one basis, carefully worked out, learned

Relationships are the blood vessels of life in our groups

and practised by every leader, for it is here that many of the barriers are broken down and the foundations laid for meaningful relationships.

Encouraging involvement and participation

People are usually most co-operative and willing to participate when they are new to a group so involvement should be encouraged right from the start. Not only will it help at a practical level but it develops the idea of a 'self help' group where everyone shares a corporate sense of responsibility. Doing things with others spurs conversation and friendships. Many a meaningful discussion has taken place whilst making coffee, rolling play dough, painting multicoloured splodges and cleaning up the mess afterwards. Some may even go on to help with administration, or to organize craft activities or even volunteer to lead singing. The possibilities are endless.

Movement around the room is another major factor in getting a group to mix and gel. Adults who remain seated on a chair will often remain static in relationships. Careful planning in the setting out of rooms can discourage the formation of small immovable groups.

Communal activities such as singing and story-telling will be most successful when all of the adults join in. My own approach is to say that if I have to sing (often out of tune!) and wave my arms around, then I need the moral support of others doing it with me. Generally speaking, it works. Whatever ground rules we make it is important to be very clear about them at the registration stage.

Getting to know you

The adults in a Parent and Toddler group have so many shared experiences related to the children in their care that conversation should never be in short supply. And these conversations give immediate insight into other important areas of life such as partners, work, hobbies, social life and holidays. It is not difficult for a leader to acquire a very full picture of the lifestyles of the group members.

Understanding differences in lifestyles is essential. Without it, we are talking *at* people, rather than *with* them and it becomes impossible to make connections between our faith and their experience. In all our dealings with those we serve it matters that we know what interests them, motivates them, worries them, disappoints and delights them. Their thinking on issues relating to life in the community, health, education, crime and punishment gives us greater understanding of them as people and with it the opportunity to apply the Christian faith in a meaningful and relevant manner.

Through prayer, listening and observation it will simply be a matter of time before we develop a personal sharing of life's anxieties too. Problems with an elderly parent, a broken relationship, serious illness, miscarriage, housing or unemployment will come to the surface quite naturally where meaningful relationships have been formed.

Many groups link a support programme with their Parent and Toddler group in order to give greater opportunity for listening, learning and discussion of relevant topics and

Talking with people, not at them

'Through Parent and Toddler groups churches are establishing links and building relationships with young families in the community, and indirectly with midwives, health visitors and social workers who are also involved in caring for them.'

(Kathleen Crawford, *Under Fives Welcome!*, Scripture Union, 1990)

Building Relationships

Starting from shared experiences

issues affecting adults and children. The aim of such times is not necessarily to 'evangelize' but to help each other explore issues and concerns relating to our lifestyles. It's a wonderful way of getting to know each other. Opportunities to present a Christian perspective may well arise and be well received. But it is important not to deceive people by using the group as a 'front', seemingly secular but behind which heavy preaching takes place. Such an approach will only be counter-productive.

Relationships take time

'Some weeks after my arrival at the toddler group my identity as 'the vicar's wife' was revealed. One mother was none too pleased and saw my presence as a real threat to her cosy little gathering. In no uncertain terms she told me that if I dared to introduce anything religious into the group they'd all either boycott the place or mount a 'take-over' bid. I don't mind admitting that I was terrified of her—she was a very forceful and influential woman. I could well believe that the entire group would follow wherever she led. There was no alternative but to make her the subject of my daily prayers. If I was to have the courage to face her each week I needed all the divine help I could get.

My prayers and goals started with things like, 'Dear Lord, I pray that she might simply look at me this week without disdain and aggression in her face.' The following week it continued, 'Oh Lord, please help me to smile at her this week.'

This continued for months and months until we really were communicating well. Neither of us could believe it. It had to be a miracle. The following year when we started to run discussion groups and were inviting people to guest services, not only was she amongst the first to come, but she made the others come too!'

(Judith Wigley, *Under Fives and their Families*, Marshall Pickering)

Building Relationships

Parent and Toddler Group Leadership

Responsibility for creating a warm and welcoming atmosphere in any Parent and Toddler group lies with the leaders. Good team work, advance planning and careful preparation will avoid many of the negative experiences often associated with this kind of group.

Consider the following five points in your leadership team:

- **ALLOW** time for prayer for yourselves as a team, the building you are using, the atmosphere that you will create and individuals who attend. Aim to pray together, albeit briefly, before the start of each session. Some groups enlist prayer support from fellow church members, who promise to pray regularly for the needs of the group.

- **ARRANGE** duty rotas in advance ensuring that all jobs are covered and the most (and least) pleasant ones are shared. Paperwork and publcity (registration, welcome information, notices and newsletters) should be prepared well ahead of time.

- **ANTICIPATE** problems that may arise (cliquishness, adults who don't 'fit in', disruptive children, unco-operative parents) and devise consistent strategies for dealing with them.

- **AVOID** letting situations build up by acting quickly and firmly, but always in a friendly manner. Do not apologize for important decisions that have been prayerfully made.

- **AIM** to bring the whole group, children and adults, together at some point during the session in order to welcome new people, give out notices and generally encourage a sense of group concern and commitment.

Practicalities

 List every job involved in running one Parent and Toddler group session from unlocking the premises at the start, to switching off the last light at the end. How is this workload to be evenly shared?

 In what ways can the layout of chairs, toys and equipment in your room/hall affect the movement and involvement of both children and adults?

 How would you tackle some of the problems listed above (and any others you can think of) should the need arise?

 How can you best use the 'group' time to communicate a spirit of interest and concern as well as fostering an atmosphere of warmth and friendship?

Notes

'That energy which makes a child hard to manage is the energy which afterward makes him a manager of life.'

Henry Ward Beecher

The Welcome Procedure

A welcome procedure should aim to achieve three things:

1. Alleviate any fears and anxieties in adults and children.

2. Communicate important information about the group.

3. Provide leaders with basic facts about the people registering.

Generally speaking, an adult bringing a child along to the group for the first time will want answers to the following questions:

? Who runs the group and which official body sponsors it?

? What actually happens at each group session?

? As I'm expected to attend with my child, what level of participation will be expected of me?

As a group discuss appropriate responses to these questions. Check your answers against the three aims. Keep that word 'welcome' in mind. Swamping newcomers with irrelevant information is almost as bad as leaving out vital facts.

- Write down the information you feel important enough to be recorded on welcome literature.

- Think carefully about the information that needs to be requested by your registration form.

- Consider the layout and content of the sample welcome literature opposite and discuss alternatives that might be more suitable for your group. How much information do you need to give? How wordy should it be? Will it need graphics or illustrations?

Remember that it is not so much what you say, but how you say it that makes all the difference!

- Be prayerful.

- Make it one-to-one.

- Invite the newcomers to sit down.

- Speak to the child/baby.

- Introduce yourself first.

- Complete registration form.

- 'Chat' through information.

- Allow them to ask questions.

- Introduce them to someone else.

- Smile and relax!

Ten Tips
for welcoming new adults and children to your group

14

Other church information for your interest.

Family Worship 10.30 am every Sunday

Creche provision for 0-2½ year olds

Scramblers for 2½-5 year olds

Climbers for 5-7 year olds

Thanksgiving and baptism enquiries: every Tuesday evening between 7.00 and 8.00 pm at the church, where clergy and staff are always available.

Friday Mornings at Green Lane Hall

9.30 - 11.15 am.

A range of discussion groups for women. There is a crèche with qualified supervision and places for up to thirty children. Futher details from any Parent and Toddler leader.

WELCOME

to Newtown Parish Church Parent and Toddler groups.
(Mondays 1.00 - 3.00pm and Wednesdays 9.30 - 11.30am) during school term.

Our Parent and Toddler groups are for children under ... years of age and their parents / accompanying adults.

As a church group we hope to provide the local community with a warm, friendly atmosphere and a safe play environment for adults, babies and small children. We operate a registration system restricting our numbers to the recommendations set out by the Children Act (1989). This is to give you and your children the highest possible standards of safety, hygiene and quality friendships. We hope that we can offer you a place at the session of your choice immediately. If that is not possible we will welcome you as a visitor for two introductory sessions, after which we must ask you to wait until a vacancy arises. Thank you for your understanding in this.

What happens at Parent and Toddler groups?

Our groups are very informal but they do have a definite structure that we find beneficial to all who attend. Below is a rough outline of a typical session. All timings are approximate.

	AM Sessions	PM Sessions
Arrive, pay subs & play	9.30 – 10.15	1.00 – 1.45
Children's drinks	10.15 – 10.30	1.45 – 2.15
Adults' drinks	10.30	2.00
Tidy and clear away	11.00	2.30
Singing time for everyone	11.05 - 11.15	2.35 - 2.45

Please do move around the hall and get to know other adults and children, especially if you have come with a friend. Do remember that many have come on their own.

What do you need to know?

1. Subscriptions are ...p per session to help cover the cost of drinks, heat and lighting, new toys and equipment. An additional charge of ...p per session is made for a second child. Visitors will be charged ...p for coffee.

2. Toilets and baby-changing facilities are along the corridor where you entered the building.

3. At least once a term please sign up to help with drinks and coffee. Someone will always be available to show you the ropes first time.

4. There will will be a regular newsletter giving details of all our termly activities and events.

NEWTOWN PARISH CHURCH PARENT AND TODDLER GROUP
REGISTRATION FORM

ADULT'S NAME: _____

RELATIONSHIP WITH CHILD: Parent / Grandparent / Childminder / Other

CHILD'S NAME(S) _____ Age _____ Date of birth _____

_____ Age _____ Date of birth _____

ADDRESS (of adult bringing child): _____

TELEPHONE: _____

_____ TELEPHONE: _____

DOCTOR: _____

OTHER PRE-SCHOOL GROUP(S) ATTENDED: _____

PLEASE STATE IN ORDER OF PREFERENCE SESSION REQUIRED:

Monday pm   Wednesday am

HAVE YOU HAD ANY PREVIOUS CONTACT WITH CHURCH:

Sunday school / Youth Group / Wedding / Baptism / Thanksgiving?

FORM COMPLETED BY: _____ DATE: _____

Building Relationships

Planning a Social Event

Giving your Parent and Toddler group a 'supporting programme' of occasional social events can act as a valuable catalyst to the important process of building relationships with adults and children. Devising the programme will require a lot of prayer, as well as careful planning and preparation. It is important to remember what you are trying to achieve by such events, and then pray and work towards that end.

Some guidelines to help your planning

- Be clear about your primary aim of providing an environment in which to build relationships.

- Don't be too ambitious: one well-organized event a year is better than six poorly-run events.

- Choose events that leave you free to be with your folk and not absorbed in organizing the whole time. If necessary involve other Christians from the church to share in the hard work at the event.

- In deciding the type of event, be influenced by the needs of your children and the interests of your adults. Don't forget to consider the interests of any men who may attend your groups. Pray about this decision.

- Think through the financial, babysitting and transport aspects of any event. If booking transport for children remember to ask the coach company about their policy on sharing seats and babies on knees.

- Consider the advantages and disadvantages of daytime or evening events, never underestimate the work and staffing involved in running creches!

- Find out what local facilities are available through the library or local authority tourist information. Consider a wider field if necessary.

Ideas for events / programmes

Daytime events focusing on the children

- *Theme picnics (indoors or out)*: teddy bears, pyjamas, princes and princesses, TV or Disney characters.

- *Seasonal parties*: Christmas, Easter, Harvest, May Day.

- *Special play experiences*: Devote a session to an activity you don't normally attempt—water play, foot and hand painting, ball pools, bouncy castles or special soft play equipment.

- *Trips out*: to a local park, the zoo, a theme park, a swimming pool, a city farm.

- *Animal visits*: carefully supervised visits from rabbits, kittens, puppies etc for the children to watch and touch.

Evening social events for adults only

- *A meal out in a restaurant*: allow adults to pay in instalments prior to the event.

- *Exercise or sports evening*: squash, circuit training, step aerobics, dance, badminton. It's possible to hire part of a leisure centre with some instruction available: this may be particularly appealing to any men in the group.

- *A hobbies/interest evening*: invite speakers on subjects such as fashion, colour co-ordination, slimming, DIY, cookery, gardening, travel, health issues. Provide a light supper.

- *Demonstration evening*: crafts, cake decorating, make-up.

Suggested themes for talk / discussion support programmes

Children's issues: feeding and diet, potty training, sleeplessness, the 'terrible twos', immunisation and illness, special needs, preparing for nursery/school, holidaying with under fives.

Women's health issues: pregnancy, miscarriage, post-natal depression, eating and slimming, Well Woman clinics, relationships.

Life issues: abortion, Aids, bereavement, education, caring for the elderly, returning to work, combining work and parenthood, child-care.

Groups regularly attended by men will undoubtedly benefit from the presence of male leaders. Where this isn't possible, it is essential to build in a 'male-friendly' element in to a supporting programme. While many of the above suggestions do not exclude men, they may prefer a couples or 'male only' event.

Dispelling the Myths

Contents

A three-page *Briefing* paper on hearing and dealing with our contacts' misconceptions about God and the Church.

Two pages of *Ideas* for prayer and praying together.

A *Discussion* exercise on identifying the myths people believe about the Christian faith.

A page of *Illustrations*: cartoon discussion starters of some basic Do's and Don'ts for running a Parent and Toddler Group.

Extras

Don't make assumptions

If building bridges for faith-sharing is on your agenda, it's just as well to make sure that you are all in agreement about basic Christian truth. There's no need to enrol at theological college, but it may be worthwhile to check through the following questions together:

- Why is Jesus unique?
- What is so special about the Bible?
- What answers do you have when friends ask why bad things happen to good people?
- How should we react when told that Christianity is just one of many equally valid 'faith options'?
- What criteria should we have for selecting songs and Bible stories?

Dispelling the Myths

One of the programmes I always try to listen to is BBC Radio 2's *Good Morning Sunday*. The presenter is Don Maclean. He succeeds in making all his listeners feel valued by showing that their opinions are of importance to the programme. He himself is a committed Christian, but judging from the letters he receives, his listeners are not only people of different faiths but also those with little or no faith or church connection. Many of the issues he discusses with the audience are God and church-related. Consequently, as I listen week by week I am provided with valuable insights into a wide range of people's thinking about God and the church.

Then you will know the truth, and the truth will set you free.

John 8:32

Surplus baggage?

The starting point of Christian witness must be listening. We need to know what, if anything, people believe and, more importantly, what it is that led them to their belief or non-belief. Whilst the 1991 English Church Census informs us that only ten per cent of the population attends church regularly, other surveys have indicated that very many more have some kind of belief in God. But the image they have is often a distorted half-picture based on a kind of folk religion or a self-created god. It is a long way from the personal, loving creator God of the Bible.

Such 'god images' will have been formed by a mixture of religious inputs, some positive but others extremely negative. Boring school assemblies, an unhappy Sunday School experience, problems encountered when trying to plan a wedding, funeral or baptism, negative media coverage of the Church as an institution (including soap opera portrayals of 'religious' people), or simply an unfriendly 'Christian' neighbour — all of these go towards feeding the already disfigured image of God in people's minds.

Our task is to unpack this baggage that has accumulated in peoples lives and in so doing dispel the many myths about God and his Church. It can feel like a very long process of clearing the way so that fresh and truthful input can replace the old and unhelpful images previously formed. But, if we are prepared for the challenge, Parent and Toddler groups are the ideal environment in which this can take place.

Be prepared to listen

People often reveal hidden thoughts about God without realizing it. And we are only able to 'hear' what is being said when we are listening prayerfully with the help of the Holy Spirit. Many casual conversations will touch on issues or subjects that give a clear indication of a person's outlook on life, not least their attitudes towards God. When sensitively and skilfully handled such conversations will uncover much more.

On occasions they can be created. One of the questions on our Parent and Toddler group registration form asks, 'Have you had any previous contact with the church?' Immediately we are establishing with the adults that we are a church group; we are learning something of their church background (if any) and, most importantly, opening up a conversation which can quite easily reveal individual reactions and feelings about the church and about God.

It is primarily a ministry of listening. The speed of development and deepening of these conversations will vary

from person to person. Some take it as an opportunity to tell you their entire family history relating to the church 'in the good old days', whilst others obviously resent being asked the question in the first place. Either way careful hearing of what is being said provides an insight into an individual's perception of God.

Our listening will also enable them to hear themselves. Many will never have explored their own thinking on such matters, let alone talked about them. It is important that our response is one that encourages that exploration, not prevents it.

Be prepared to demonstrate the truth

Jesus' own ministry on earth embraced both the demonstration and declaration of the Kingdom of God and it was often his actions that drew attention to his words. People couldn't fail to notice the way in which he spoke to the lonely and outcast of society as well as bringing comfort and healing to the sick. He practised what he preached. For us in our Parent and Toddler groups the most powerful demonstration of the gospel will come through what we do and the way in which we do it. People like Mother Theresa have influenced thousands of lives in this way.

Many distorted truths about Christians, the Church and God will be slowly amended through our demonstration of his true character. Past negative experiences will be replaced with positive ones which will encourage healthy images of God. For those with little or no understanding or experience of God and his people this is an important part of their learning process. It is here that they will begin to learn that God is loving, caring, accepting and interested in them as individuals. It is at this stage that others will begin to change and

modify their own misconceptions. As the Holy Spirit works through us we have the privilege of witnessing a softening of attitudes and the beginnings of growth as the image of the true God as we know him replaces the old.

Be prepared to speak the truth

Speaking about God and our experience of him should arise quite naturally out of our demonstration of his love. The opportunities will often come when we are least expecting them and will demand a wide variety of responses. Too often we have a fixed impression of what we ought to be saying, rather than responding naturally to what is being asked or simply correcting a distorted picture. A ten minute delivery on how we came to Christ or a three-point mini sermon on the cross is unlikely to be an appropriate response within the framework of a Parent and Toddler group—but don't bypass them should the situation demand!

All the same, we are more likely to be required to express an opinion on

---

Think of all the different sorts of family which may be represented in a group of children.

Their homes may be:

Christian, atheist, agnostic, academic, wealthy, poor.

Their homes may be places where the television is watched all the time
 – or where people go out a lot to the theatre or to concerts.

They may be children whose every desire is met
 – or those who are treated worse than the furniture.

Their parents may not care about the future of their children
 – or they may have high aspirations for them.

The children may have attended playgroup or nursery school.

(Penny Frank, *Children & Evangelism*, Marshall Pickering)

Dispelling the Myths

a national tragedy, explain something about a Christian festival, comment on a current issue affecting the Church or gently correct a grossly exaggerated rumour about the vicar's baptism policy (or the roof appeal)!

As our friendships develop into mutual trust and respect, we will feel an increasing confidence in talking about the ways in which we conduct our lives and the part that God plays in

them. An honest account of how we spent our weekend or how we cope with endless sleepless nights will provide natural opportunities to speak about God. In this way we are bringing him into the real world. Being willing and prepared to speak about him is crucial and is best learned by doing it! The Holy Spirit is a wonderful teacher and will never fail to hear the prayers of those wanting to learn to speak about him.

> *The reason why we have two ears and only one mouth is that we may listen the more and talk the less.*
>
> **Zeno of Citium (300 AD)**

Understanding the community in which the church is set helps prevent false assumptions being made about people. Understanding the traditions and social history of an area provides vital clues to people's attitudes - including their attitude to the Christian Gospel. This is a fundamental approach in the missionary enterprise which we cannot bypass: understanding the culture which is so often locked into the history of the area.

Care needs to be taken in getting as clear a picture as possible of the overall situation in the community. It was for this reason that we spent a good proportion of our time in our first few months at All Saints auditing the community and the congregation. Ever since then understanding our community has been a continuous priority. Even after the original surveys and audits we have continued to seek to understand the area in which we live.

(Mike Breen, *Growing the Smaller Church*, Marshall Pickering)

Dispelling the Myths

Praying

Any form of evangelism is a threat to the territory of our enemy and will lead us into a confrontational ministry. The very nature of Parent and Toddler groups takes God out into the community in an exciting way, influencing people and places with the message of the gospel. That must be a worrying thought for the devil.

Paul reminds us in his letter to the church at Ephesus that 'our struggle is not against flesh and blood, but against the rulers, against the authorities, against the powers of this dark world and against the spiritual forces of evil in the heavenly realms.' (Ephesians 6:12) We are engaged in battle and need to equip ourselves with God's armour through prayer. Without him all our efforts will be in vain. No amount of good organization, hard work or brilliant ideas will bear fruit unless God is at the centre.

Jesus said: 'Remain in me and I will remain in you. No branch can bear fruit by itself; it must remain in the vine. Neither can you bear fruit unless you remain in me.' (John 15:4) Prayer is our vine line!

- **Pray for yourselves as leaders and for your families**. Ask for health, strength and protection in order to do the work that you are called to.

- **Pray that you will become leaders who listen to what God is saying**. Pray that you will learn to sense his will and direction for your group. Give yourself time and space in order to do this, especially before making decisions.

- **Pray together.** If possible at the start of every group session. However brief the time available, invite God to be with you and work in you each time you meet. Share the responsibility of leading that time, each taking it in turn.

- **Pray in as many different ways as you can.** Individually, in pairs, small groups and all together. Be determined, however chaotic it might feel, to pray. Don't be frightened about using set prayers or writing your own for the group to use.

- **Pray that the wider church will pray for the work.** Keep them informed with regular prayer leaflets giving information of your activities and needs.

- **Pray specifically about matters that concern you.** Ask God to give you wisdom and discernment concerning these things. Nothing is too small to matter to God.

- **Pray for individuals who come to the group.** Agree together as leaders whom each of you should pray for over a certain period of time.

- **Pray with individuals if you feel it is appropiate.** Many adults and children in real need welcome a sensitive offer of prayer and will appreciate being told that you are remembering them in your prayers.

Do not be anxious about anything, but in everything by prayer and petition, with thanksgiving, present your requests to God.

Philipians 4:6

Pray in the Spirit on all occasions and with all kinds of prayers and requests.

Ephesians 6:18

Notes

Pray in chains

Setting up a prayer chain was undoubtedly the most successful means of corporate prayer that we ever experienced as a team. The basic discipline of praying on a chain is as follows: receive your message, ring the message through to the next straight away, then pray. Our own pre-arranged times were always geared to the children's morning television programme in order to give us some time and space.

To set up a chain form a list of all those who want to be included in the chain and place at the top the team leader who will be responsible for sending the regular messages down....

Many prayers were answered through our prayer chains. One in particular stands out in my mind. Our pram services were held monthly, and despite service cards with the dates on many simply forgot. It was Monday morning preceding the pram service. God seemed to be reminding me of one particular Mum called Julie. She had only been once before. I had no idea where she lived, or even her second name. So I had no means of reminding her. So down the prayer chain went the message, 'Pray for Julie, that she will come along today.'

That afternoon, in walked Julie. One of the team welcomed her saying how good it was to see her again and asking how she had remembered. 'Oh,' came the reply, 'I didn't! My little girl was watching Playschool (on television) this morning and came out to ask me if we could go to that church where they sang and danced! Then I looked for the card that you gave me last time and discovered that it was today.'

Coincidence? God used that little girl at the exact time the request to pray for Julie passed down the telephone lines. Five years later that same Julie heads up the Parent and Toddler team as well as being a member of the pram service team itself. God hears our prayers wherever, whenever and however they are said. And here he answered with a resounding 'Yes!'

(Judith Wigley, *Under Fives and their Families*, Marshall Pickering)

Dispelling the Myths

Notes

Myth—the target!

God is a personal and private matter - not to be spoken about.

God is out of date - he has no relevance today.

God? Who or what is that?

God is a killjoy.

God isn't interested in me.

God is for the elderly, sick or dying.

God is for religious fanatics.

Dispelling the myths

 1 How common are the attitudes shown here in the adults who attend your Parent and Toddler group? How do they usually express them?

Are you aware of any other 'myths' held by your group members?

How are these mistaken messages passed on to the next generation?

 2 In what ways is the Church guilty of projecting these images?

 3 Are we as Parent and Toddler group leaders in danger of reinforcing such impressions? How might what we say and do be misinterpreted?

 4 Without becoming overly self-conscious, what can we do to help dispel some of these myths?

SPOT THE DIFFERENCE

Compare these two scenes and compile your own list of practical do's and don'ts for your group.

Evangelistic Opportunities

Contents

A three-page *Briefing* paper on developing personal contacts for evangelism.

A *Discussion* sheet on gossiping the gospel.

An *Ideas* sheet on planning an evangelistic event.

Two page *Discussion* on knowing, understanding and telling your own story of faith.

Useful addresses for evangelistic speakers:

CPAS
Evangelism Division
Athena Drive
Tachbrook Park
WARWICK
CV34 6NG
(0926) 334242

Maranatha Ministries
Christian Teaching Centre
KIRKBY STEPHEN
Cumbria
CA17 4ES

Christian Viewpoint
14 Parkfield Road
STOURBRIDGE
West Midlands
DY8 1HD
(0384) 370775
(0732) 460625

Diocesan evangelists
Many dioceses employ evangelists or missioners. Contact your local diocesan office.

Extras

No bed of roses

Sharing one's faith can bring great joy. But it has to be admitted that it can also bring pain and heartache. Penny Frank offers the following 'Facts to accept about evangelism'. As a group, discuss you reactions to them.

- Evangelism is tough and can be totally and bewilderingly unrewarding.
- We proclaim the Gospel because it is true.
- We proclaim it in a way which is appropriate for the type and age of person who is listening to us because we really want them to understand.
- There is never any guarantee of success.

Evangelistic Opportunities

Welcome to those who have jumped to this chapter first. I've done it myself in other books on evangelism—scanned the chapter titles and index quickly and then turned to the section that I think has the practical suggestions in answer to all my evangelism problems. It's what I call the 'technique trap'. There's nothing wrong with learning a skill, acquiring useful information, or benefiting from others' experiences as long as we remember that these things are aids to our evangelism and not answers in themselves.

Events will never substitute for our individual desire to speak about Jesus

Evangelism is someONE and not something

Bishop Michael Marshall, of the Archbishop of Canterbury's *Springboard* initiative for the Decade of Evangelism, insists that evangelism is *someone* not *something*. Effective evangelism stems from our willingness and desire to share the person of Jesus. We may not all be called to be evangelists in the sense of having a specific responsibility to persuade people to turn to Christ (although some of us will!) but we are all called to be witnesses to him.

Jesus himself—what he has done for us and what he means to us in our everyday lives—will be the single most powerful tool for evangelism with our Parent and Toddler group members. Our motivation at this level will be the driving force behind any planning of group or larger meetings. Such events in themselves will never substitute for our individual desire to speak about Jesus.

Evangelism should be, first and foremost, personal

As a young Christian I experienced quite a bit of hostility towards my faith from people who were close to me. Talking about God caused tension amd unhappiness and I learned very quickly to avoid it. Consequently I became very skilled at holding back in normal everyday conversation—almost to the point of being dishonest. In reply to a simple question such as, 'What did you do on Saturday?' I'd say, 'Shopping with friends.' But in reality the shopping, which took ten minutes, had been to buy supplies for the evangelistic coffee bar where I'd spent almost six hours of my Saturday!

It has taken me years to learn to relax and allow my faith to show quite naturally in public, not worrying about what people think of me. It is never a surprise to me to discover that the most effective evangelists in our Parent and Toddler groups are those who have recently become Christians. Their freshness and spontaneity in 'gossiping the gospel' is a joy to watch. Many of us who have been Christians for a long time need to pray that God will restore that freshness, reminding us of our first love and with it renew our motivation to share Jesus in our everyday conversations. Parent and Toddler groups will provide us with endless ongoing opportunities for doing so.

> *The first thing we need to discover is that there is no thing to discover. There is no such thing as the gospel. For the gospel is not a thing, it is a person: it is Jesus and his resurrection. For the gospel is not a formula or a text or a code; otherwise, it could have been communicated without getting involved in the whole messy business of the incarnation. An angel or a telegram would have sufficed! The message and the messenger are one. Jesus is the gospel: the gospel is Jesus.*
>
> (Michael Marshall, *The Gospel Connection*, DLT)

We may need to spend time thinking and praying about our witness, admitting our fears and anxieties concerning what people think about us. We will need to get down to learning how to share our faith effectively so that we can make the most of the natural situations that do arise.

Evangelism should be varied in its approach

The members of our Parent and Toddler groups will vary in their understanding of our individual witness to Jesus—and in their receptivity to it. The privilege of our regular ongoing contact with them is that we are able to be sensitive and discerning in our approach, adapting it according to the situation that we are in.

In the parable of the sower (Mark 4:3-20) Jesus explained graphically how the different types of ground on which the seed landed represent the varying responses in people who 'hear' the message. One of our tasks is to prepare the ground for that message. Through our personal contact and understanding of where people are we should be able to gauge a group or an event accordingly.

Acknowledging and respecting an individual's 'journey of faith' is important. We must be sure not to dismiss what small flame of faith might already be there. Nor should we fall into the trap of pushing people too far, too soon and causing them to stop 'travelling' altogether.

There will also always be those who will never allow the seeds to settle on their heart's ground, as the parable of the sower clearly indicates. No single event will ever meet the needs of a whole group, nor should we expect it to. Different events will achieve different things. With prayer and careful planning we should be able to sense the right time for the right evangelistic approach.

Evangelism should begin where they are

Having already acknowledged that everyone will be at a different stage in their spiritual journeying, we need also to remember that the majority of these travellers will not be in the mainstream of church life. Their culture and lifestyle will not necessarily embrace what is so familiar to most Christians. For many, the styles of music and language of an average Sunday service will involve a major culture shock.

We need to take such factors into account when planning our evangelistic events. The time and place should be geared deliberately to their needs, not ours. High quality facilities for the children should always be a priority, especially when running crèches.

We should always remember that we are usually contacting only one part of a family unit. Encouraging group members to talk with their partners about what they have heard is very important. Men can sometimes feel resentful because, as they see it, their partners are being drawn into something 'religious'. While we wouldn't want to hold anyone back who is ready to make a commitment to Christ, we should also help them to bring those whom they love with them on their journey. It may be possible to develop a strategy for witnessing to men with the help of group leaders' husbands or other men in the church. But by far the most effective witness will happen when couples befriend other couples.

A sensitive and discerning approach

Evangelistic Opportunities

Now we see how such pathetic questions as, 'Do we need to mention his name?' or, 'In what ways do we refer to the particularity of Jesus in evangelistic, gospel presentations?' find their level. If we believe that the essential ingredient in all evangelism in all its forms is the real presence of Jesus, then surely we behave with the same courteous, warm, and loving attention that we show when we take anyone with us to a party or to a place. We do not ignore them. We do not call him or her 'it', but rather we call them by their name. We introduce them and tell people enough about them to enable such a connection to be formed that a relationship may begin. Admittedly, much of this presentation is verbal, though it generally involves touch and shaking of hands, hospitality (food and drink), and generally sharing our friends with other friends and acquaintances.

If we are truly at home with that friend in an easy, natural friendship (John 15:15), then there will be nothing unreal, unnatural, pompous, or pretentious about the tones in which we speak of some of our friends to others of our friends. On the contrary, there is something real in what we say because Jesus is really present by the Holy Spirit, and, according to his promise, 'where two or three are gathered in my name, there am I in the midst of them.' (Matthew 18:20)

(Michael Marshall, *The Gospel Connection*, DLT)

Evangelistic Opportunities

Gossiping the Gospel

Being honest and open in our everyday conversation will almost inevitably lead to us speaking about our beliefs and experience of God. It shouldn't be an embarrassing, buttonholing, pressurizing conversation but simply us speaking honestly and naturally about our faith in a way that is informative, relevant and helpful to our friends and contacts.

Look at this conversation between Jenny, a Parent and Toddler group member, and Jackie, one of the leaders:

Hello, Jenny. Did you have a good weekend?

Yes thanks.

Do anything exciting?

Well, it was quite quiet really, although we did manage to take the kids swimming on Saturday and we went to my mum and dad for dinner on Sunday. Nothing like mum's dinners and they like to see the baby.

Sounds good to me...we all had lunch at church this week. Not quite the same as your mum's Sunday dinner, I'm sure, but it was really good fun and the children think it's great being able to sit with all their friends for a meal. I quite like the church picnics myself, when the weather's good of course!

You might not think that there is anything special about that conversation, but very simply and naturally it achieves three important things:

- It tells Jenny that church is a natural part of Jackie's life.

- It communicates the fact that the children love it.

- It lets Jenny know that being with other Christians can be fun!

The conversation may not go any further but it has arisen through everyday chatter and is an important beginning to Christian witness. Some conversations will give a much greater opportunity for Christian input especially as we grow in our relationships with people and become more confident about sharing. Some will occur quite naturally while others will be initiated by us.

Getting started

In twos or threes consider how the possible conversation starters (opposite) from group members could be developed.

Ask yourself three things:

- What might be the feelings behind each statement?

- Does this tell me anything about how they see life or God?

- How can I respond honestly and appropiately as a Christian taking into consideration the factors discussed in the first two questions?

'James is getting me up three or four times a night at the moment, I just can't cope.'

'Mary's had a boy. I saw them yesterday. He's perfect, a real little miracle.'

'Our house sale has just fallen through. It obviously wasn't meant to be.'

'Joan's had a miscarriage. She's really upset and keeps saying she feels so empty. I don't know what to say.'

'It's brilliant being able to shop on Sundays, Tom can come with me.'

'I could barely listen to the news today—there's been another child murder. I don't know what's happening to the world.'

'My father-in-law has been told he has cancer and he's only 56 years old.'

'We've decided to get married now that Ben is born. I want the security now.'

4 Evangelistic Opportunities

Planning an evangelistic event

There are two very important questions every Parent and Toddler group should ask when planning an evangelistic event:

1. When is the time right?   *2. What is the most appropiate kind of event?*

Only you as leaders will be able to make these important decisions. Here are some guidelines and suggestions to help you.

What kind of event?

Here are five suggestions of different kinds of evangelistic events that you might like to try specifically for Parent and Toddler group members when you feel the time is right.

- **Enquirers discussion groups**. These should be advertised with the very clear intention of discussing issues relating to the Christian faith. Ideally there should be no more than seven or eight in a group. They can be geared to the needs of those attending, with meetings on 'neutral territory' or even in a group member's home. Daytime groups will require a crèche. Evening groups should invite partners to attend.

- **Guest Services / Seeker Services**. These are appropiate only to those who are able and ready to come into the church building and cope with a degree of church culture. Careful planning with church leaders will help to make the service a relevant and positive experience. Sermon themes such as 'Our children's future' and 'Parenthood in the 1990s' may well draw people in. Quality care and involvement for children should be a priority and made clear on any invitations.

- **A 'Speaker' event**. There may be enough interest among your Parent and Toddler group members to warrant a special evening or daytime event on 'neutral ground' using a carefully chosen evangelistic speaker. A Christian celebrity from sport or show business can make a tremendous impact, but what really matters is finding someone who can make the gospel make sense to your particular audience.

- **Pram services / All-age activity learning times**. These are invaluble times of learning for adults and children and should never be underestimated in their evangelistic influence. Bible stories, prayer and worship are experienced at an unthreatening level at a time and place convenient to group members. When run on a regular basis they demand a lot of energy and resources, but can be equally fruitful as occasional events, linked to Christmas, Easter or Harvest.

- **A video event**. This is probably the least demanding to set up and can be adapted to suit a wide range of people. Recent years have seen an increase in the availability of good quality Christian videos featuring the testimonies of some remarkable people. There are also some excellent 'Christian Apologetics' programmes. An informal group of this kind may well be prepared to move on to watching and discussing the *Christian Basics* videos suitable for an enquirers' group.

The planning of any kind of evangelistic event will require a lot of prayer, advance preparations, well thought-out publicity and invitations, combined with a strategy for follow-up.

Timing

Ask yourselves:

- **Do we have good individual relationships with our group members? Do they know we are Christians? Have we had one-to-one conversations with them about our faith?**

- **What are the practical restrictions upon their lifestyles? Is daytime or evening more suitable? Do they have older children or extended family resposibilities? What would be the response of their partner to them attending such an event?**

- **What time of year is most suitable for group members? Do we have the manpower and resources to make the event a success? Have we considered the cost in terms of facilities, leadership, publicity, crèche helpers, finance?**